GO FACTS ANIMALS
Mammals

A & C BLACK • LONDON

Mammals

contents

First published 2002 in Australia by Blake Education Pty Ltd

This edition published 2003 in the United Kingdom by
A&C Black Publishers Ltd, 37 Soho Square, London W1D 3QZ
www.acblack.com

ISBN 0-7136-6605-6

A CIP record for this book is available from the British Library.

Written by Paul McEvoy
Science Consultant: Sandy Ingleby, Division of Vertebrate Zoology
(Mammals), Australian Museum
Design and layout by The Modern Art Production Group
Photos by Photodisc, Stockbyte, John Foxx, Corbis, Imagin,
Artville and Corel

UK Series Consultant: Julie Garnett

Printed in Hong Kong by Wing King Tong Co Ltd

A & C Black uses paper produced with elemental chlorine-free pulp,
harvested from managed sustainable forests.

4		**What is a Mammal?**
10		**Mammals with Hoofs**
12		**Carnivores**
14		**Monkeys and Apes**
16		**Sea Mammals**
18		**Rodents**
20		**Flying Mammals**
22	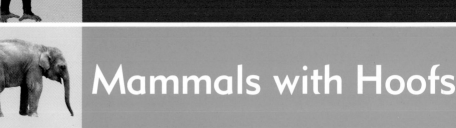	**How Mammals Move**
23		**Glossary and Index**

Mammals are warm-blooded animals that have a backbone. Mammals are the only animals that feed their babies with mother's milk.

All mammals are warm-blooded. That means they keep the same body temperature all the time. Keeping warm uses up a lot of energy, so mammals need more food than **cold-blooded** animals such as reptiles.

Most mammals are covered with fur or hair. The fur helps to keep the animals warm. Sea mammals without fur, such as whales, have a layer of fat to keep them warm.

Mammals give birth to live babies. The mother **suckles** her babies, making milk to feed them. Milk is a special food that helps the young mammal to grow.

Black panthers
are meat-eaters.

Brown bears eat
meat but also eat
fruits and seeds.

Elephants use
their large ears
to keep cool.

Types of Mammals

There are over 4 000 types of mammals. They come in many shapes and sizes.

Mammals can be as small as your finger or as big as a whale. Humans are mammals, which means that you are a mammal.

Some mammals eat other animals. They are **carnivores**. Lions are mammals that hunt and eat animals.

Some mammals eat grass or other plants. They are **herbivores**. A rhinoceros is a mammal that eats plants.

Mammals live in all parts of the world. You will find mammals from the hottest desert to the coldest pole. Some mammals live in the ocean, and some can even fly.

Whales are mammals that live in the ocean.

Bats are mammals that can fly like birds.

Life Cycle of a Mammal

How a mammal grows from a baby to an adult.

1 A baby mammal develops inside its mother.

2 After it is born, a baby mammal needs to be cared for. The baby suckles on milk from its mother. At first, the milk is all the food the baby needs.

3 As it grows larger, a baby mammal learns to feed itself.

4 A young adult can look after itself. It leaves its parents to look for a mate.

1

2

4

3

Mammals with hoofs eat plants. They are herbivores. Zebras, giraffes and elephants are all mammals with hoofs.

Many hoofed mammals live in groups called herds. They often live on open plains or grasslands. The herd moves from place to place in search of food. Zebras and wildebeest live in large herds.

Hoofed mammals are plant-eaters. Plant-eaters have flat, wide teeth to grind their food. Zebras and wildebeest eat grass. Giraffes and elephants eat leaves.

Elephants are the largest land animals. They live in family groups called herds. Baby elephants feed on mother's milk for two years while they grow.

Elephants protect their young.

Giraffes are the tallest land animals.

Wildebeest live in large herds.

Elephants pull down trees. They create large areas of grassland.

Mammal	Number of species
elephants	2
antelopes	54
zebras	3

Carnivores

Mammals that are carnivores hunt and eat other animals. Lions, tigers and foxes are carnivores.

Lions and tigers are the largest of the big cats. They hunt and eat other animals for food. They use their sharp teeth and claws to catch and kill their food.

Lions live in a family group called a **pride**. The baby lions feed on milk. As they grow, they learn to hunt for themselves. Lions kill and eat zebras, antelope and other mammals.

Foxes hunt and eat other animals. They use their sharp teeth to catch and eat their food. Foxes kill and eat birds, **rodents** and other small animals.

A lion can jump on its prey.

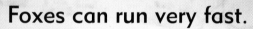

Foxes can run very fast.

Tigers can swim.

HUNTER!

A lion can catch an animal twice its size.

Mammal	Number of species
big cats	7
foxes	21

Monkeys and Apes

Monkeys and apes are mammals called primates. They are warm-blooded, furry animals that suckle their young.

Monkeys and apes live in tropical forests and jungles. They eat mainly nuts, seeds, fruit and leaves.

baboon

Baboons, mandrills and howlers are all monkeys. Monkeys are very good climbers. They use their hands, feet and tails to help them climb.

Apes are larger than monkeys. Chimpanzees, gibbons, orangutans and gorillas are all apes. Apes do not have tails.

Gorillas are the largest of all the apes. They live in family groups. Baby gorillas feed on milk while they are young.

14

Monkeys carry their young.

The top male gorilla in a group is called a silverback.

Orangutans are the second largest ape.

LOUDEST!

Howler monkeys are the loudest animal in the Amazon rainforest.

Mammal	Number of species
monkeys	181
apes	15

Sea Mammals

Whales, dolphins and seals are sea mammals. They are warm-blooded animals that live in the sea and feed their babies milk.

Sea mammals have flippers instead of legs. Dolphins and seals use their flippers, strong bodies and tails to swim through the water. They can swim very fast. Dolphins and seals have sharp teeth. They use them to catch fish and squid.

The blue whale is the largest animal to ever live. Blue whales feed on tiny sea creatures called **krill**. Blue whales have a layer of fat under their skin called **blubber**. The blubber helps to keep them warm in the cold water.

Whales live in groups called pods.

Killer whales are good hunters.

Dolphins have sharp teeth for catching fish.

GO FACTS

LARGEST!

The sperm whale is the largest carnivore on Earth.

Mammal	Number of species
whales and dolphins	77
seals and sea lions	34

Rodents

Rodents are small mammals with four sharp front teeth. They are warm-blooded, furry animals that suckle their young.

Rodents live in almost every part of the world, from the freezing **Arctic** to the desert. Lemmings live in the Arctic, squirrels live in forests and parks, and gerbils live in the desert. Rodents form the largest mammal group. There are more than 1700 types of rodents.

Rats, mice, squirrels and prairie dogs are all rodents. Rodents feed on grass, seeds, nuts and plants. They have sharp front teeth to help them gnaw through hard nut shells and bark. Beavers and porcupines are rodents too.

beaver

18

Prairie dogs live in large groups called townships.

Squirrels use their sharp claws to climb trees.

Porcupines are covered with long, sharp spines.

GO FACTS

DID YOU KNOW?

Almost half of all mammals are rodents.

Mammal	Number of species
rodents	1 793

Bats are the only mammals that can fly. They are warm-blooded, furry animals that suckle their young.

Bats are flying mammals, but they do not have feathers like birds. They have wings of skin that stretch from their fingers to their feet.

Many bats eat insects which they hunt at night. These bats make sounds that bounce off objects. Bats use the echoes to help them find and catch insects, such as moths, in midair.

Some bats eat fruit. These fruit bats also feed at night. They have large eyes to help them see in the dark.

Bats may fly a long
way to find food.

This long-eared
bat has very
good hearing.

A fruit bat can see
well in the dark.

21

How Mammals Move

	Walks	Swims	Climbs	Flies
lion	✓		✓	
seal		✓		
monkey	✓		✓	
bat				✓

Glossary

Arctic	very cold area near the North Pole
blubber	a layer of fat under the skin of sea mammals
carnivore	an animal that eats meat
cold-blooded	having blood that warms and cools with the surroundings
herbivore	an animal that eats plants
krill	tiny shrimp-like animals that live in the sea
pride	a group of lions
primates	a group of animals including humans, monkeys and apes
rodent	small mammals with long, sharp teeth
suckle	to feed on milk from the mother's body

Index

backbone 4

carnivore 6, 12

fur 4, 14, 18, 20

herbivore 6, 10

herd 10

humans 6

life cycle 8

primates 14

sea mammals 4, 16

suckle 4, 8, 14, 18, 20

warm-blooded 4, 14, 16, 18, 20